BASEBALL HALL OF **FAMERS**

Yogi Berra

Debra A. Estock

the rosen publishing group's
rosen central

This book is dedicated to my dad,
who early on, instilled in me a love and appreciation
for the game of baseball that remains today.

Published in 2003 by The Rosen Publishing Group, Inc.
29 East 21st Street, New York, NY 10010

The publisher has generously given permission to use extended quotations from the following copyrighted work. *When You Come to a Fork in the Road, Take It!* by Yogi Berra, with Dave Kaplan. Copyright © 2001 by Hyperion Press. Reprinted with permission of the publisher.

Library of Congress Cataloging-in-Publication Data

Estock, Debra A.
Yogi Berra / by Debra A. Estock — 1st ed.
    p. cm. — (Baseball Hall of Famers)
Summary: A biography of the ballplayer known as widely for his unusual way with words as for his skill as a catcher, batter, and manager, set against the background of the times in which he lived and played.
Includes bibliographical references and index.
ISBN 0-8239-3605-8 (lib. bdg.)
1. Berra, Yogi, 1925—Juvenile literature. 2. Baseball players—United States—Biography—Juvenile literature. 3. Baseball coaches—United States—Biography—Juvenile literature.
[1. Berra, Yogi, 1925– 2. Baseball players.]
I. Title. II. Series.
GV865.B4 E88 2003
796.357'092—dc21
                                                                2002002371

Manufactured in the United States of America

Contents

Yankees catcher and slugger Yogi Berra was one of the most successful baseball players in history. With the New York Yankees, he won ten World Series rings and fourteen American League pennants.

Introduction

Yogi Berra is a Baseball Hall of Famer and a baseball poet. Even though Berra was a super ballplayer, some people know more about what Berra says (or even doesn't say) than they do about his baseball accomplishments. The witticisms of Lawrence Peter "Yogi" Berra can pepper any conversation in which famous sports sayings are the topic of discussion. In fact, Yogi has attained almost cult status for his bon mots. He is quoted more often in *Bartlett's Familiar Quotations* than any other sports figure in history.

"It ain't over 'til it's over," "It's déjà vu all over again," "Baseball is 90 percent mental, the other half is physical," and "You can observe a lot by watching," are but a few of many classic lines attributed to the unorthodox New York Yankees catcher.

Berra was able to shine in a Yankees lineup that already boasted such greats as Joe DiMaggio, Mickey Mantle, and Roger Maris.

Berra was also a fourteen-time pennant winner and ten-time world champion. After nearly twenty years in baseball as a player and a pennant-winning manager, Berra continues to provide a unique brand of inspiration and wisdom that makes him a true American icon.

Many people think that baseball is one of the most demanding sports. It has been said that the hardest thing to do is to hit a round baseball—especially one traveling at more than 90 miles per hour—with a round bat. It may be one of the most difficult sports to play, but countless kids have lived for the dream of playing professional baseball.

Yogi Berra and his boyhood pals began playing baseball on the grass-covered fields and dusty back lots of South St. Louis, Missouri, where they lived. Baseball, in its professional form, had been around for just under fifty years. The first World Series was played in 1903. The Boston Pilgrims of the American League were pitted against the Pittsburgh Pirates of the National League.

The longtime theory of baseball has been that it is a cross between the two British games of cricket and rounders. Some historians think it was developed in 1839 by Abner Doubleday in Cooperstown, New York. Cooperstown is the quiet little village that now houses the National Baseball Hall of Fame.

Alexander J. Cartwright is known as the father of baseball and is credited with drafting the game's early rules.

This version of baseball's beginnings is the one that people at the Baseball Hall of Fame continue to tell. However, other baseball historians believe that baseball's origins actually date to 1842, when several men began playing the game in New York. They formed a team called the New York Knickerbockers. Alexander Joy Cartwright, a New York City bank cashier, surveyor, draftsman, and volunteer firefighter, is said to have adapted the game's basic rules. He is also credited with having established dimensions for a diamond-shaped field.

Until then, players had been using a square-shaped field. According to some historians, Cartwright laid out the infield, defined foul lines, and installed three bases (canvas bags filled with sand or sawdust set forty-two paces apart). He also placed an iron plate at the foot of the diamond that would serve as home base. His plan called for nine fielders—a pitcher, catcher, three basemen on the infield, a short fielder, and three outfielders. The short fielder is what we now call the shortstop.

This version of baseball had different rules, some of which were derived from cricket. Pitchers threw underhand and could run forward to release the ball from a distance of only 45 feet. Eventually, the distance between the batter and the pitcher became sixty feet, six inches, where it remains today.

Rather than throw the ball at a runner to get him out, fielders were required to throw the ball to the bases or tag the runner or hitter (called a "striker"). Players could catch a ball on the fly or on one bounce. A ball that traveled past the line of the diamond on the first- or third-base sides was considered foul, and not in play. Previously, as in cricket, once a ball was hit, it was always playable.

Alexander Cartwright wrote down twenty rules for his professional Base Ball club. He established the authority of the umpire to keep control of the game and record all violations. Two team members were designated as captains. They began the game by choosing sides for the match.

The bases were set an equal distance from one another. From home to second base was forty-two paces. From first to third base, another forty-two paces. The rules allowed that non-Knickerbocker members could be substituted to make up the nine members on each side. The winner of the game was required to record twenty-one counts or aces. The ball was required to be pitched, not thrown, for the bat. In 1857, baseball changed to a standard nine-inning format. Bases were set 90 feet apart and the umpires were given the authority to call strikes and balls.

In the mid-1880s, pitchers began to throw the ball overhand. By 1893, the mound was moved back from home plate to the present-day distance of 60 feet, 6 inches.

The forerunners of today's major leagues were organized before the turn of the nineteenth century. In 1876, William Hulbert, the owner of the Chicago White Stockings of the National Association, and seven other owners formed their own league. The eight charter members of the new National League of Professional Base Ball Clubs were Boston, Chicago, Cincinnati, St. Louis, Hartford, New York, Philadelphia, and Louisville. Rules were strictly enforced. Beer was not sold at games and the players were not allowed to drink, on or off the field. Ticket prices were 50¢ and games were prohibited on Sundays.

Clubs that were not accepted into the fledgling National League formed a new league in 1882. It was called the American Base Ball Association. It was made up of teams from Cincinnati, Louisville, St. Louis, Pittsburgh, Philadelphia, and Baltimore. In contrast to the more conservative National League, it cost only 25¢ to watch a game. Teams were allowed to play on Sundays. To the delight of many fans, they could buy liquor at ball games.

In 1901, minor league team owner Ban Johnson saw his chance to cash in on the popularity of big time baseball. He formed teams in Boston, Philadelphia, Baltimore, and Washington under the banner of the American League. In addition to offering low admission prices, Johnson knew he also had to provide quality playing on the field to draw fans. He picked up star players by raiding National League rosters. He promised them an average of $500 more per season than they were making. One-hundred eleven National Leaguers jumped to the new American League.

The National League owners were angry. They threatened legal action against Johnson, whose league became an overwhelming success. Bad feelings between the leagues continued for the next two years. But by 1903, the National League owners gave up and signed an agreement calling for a truce between the warring leagues.

The rivalry that developed in those early days remains just as strong today. Each generation of baseball lovers passionately vows allegiance to either the American League or the National League style of baseball.

The catcher has the most dangerous and least glamorous position on a baseball team. Yogi Berra, with his flair and charisma, as well as talent and skills, transformed forever the role of the baseball catcher.

The Tools of Ignorance

It may look easy to a casual spectator, but the catcher has one of the most difficult positions in baseball. Until Cartwright's standard of nine players took effect, two catchers had been stationed behind the batter. As with the other fielders, the lone catcher wore no glove and caught the ball with bare hands.

Rule changes dictated that the final strike, including a foul tip, had to be caught on a fly for a putout. This forced catchers to move closer and closer to the plate, putting them more at risk for injury. In the early days of baseball, catchers were expected to be tough. So when they began to protect themselves from injury by wearing protective clothing, they were scorned.

The first documented evidence of a catcher wearing a glove was recorded in about 1870, when Cincinnati's Doug Allison wore a pair of buckskin mittens to protect his hands. By 1890, catchers began to wear simple padded gloves.

Catchers also began to wear rubber mouth protectors, perhaps inspired by the sport of bare-knuckle boxing. The mouth protector was a forerunner to the catcher's mask. The mask was invented in 1876 by Ivy Leaguer Fred Thayer who modified a fencing mask into a wire face protector for the Harvard catcher.

Next came the chest protector. It appears that the wife of Detroit Tigers catcher Charles Bennett devised a chest pad to protect her husband from the dangers of his profession. He reportedly wore the contraption outside his jersey in 1886. While some accounts say that catchers experimented with chest protectors much earlier in the decade, it is quite likely that the catchers decided it was better to hide the padding beneath their uniforms so no one would tease them.

There are 254 members in the National Baseball Hall of Fame in Cooperstown, New York. Only thirteen catchers have been worthy of baseball's highest honor.

Catchers in the Hall of Fame	Years Played	Teams	Year of Election
Buck Ewing	1880–97	New York Giants (NL), Cleveland Spiders (NL) Cincinnati Reds (NL)	1939
Roger Bresnahan	1897–1915	Washington Senators (NL), Chicago Orphans (NL) Baltimore Orioles (AL), New York Giants (NL) St. Louis Cardinals (NL), Chicago Cubs (NL)	1945
Mickey Cochrane	1925–37	Philadelphia Athletics (AL), Detroit Tigers (AL)	1947
Bill Dickey	1928–46	New York Yankees (AL)	1954
Gabby Hartnett	1922–41	Chicago Cubs (NL), New York Giants (NL)	1955
Ray Schalk	1912–29	Chicago White Sox (AL), New York Giants (NL)	1955
Roy Campanella	1948–57	Brooklyn Dodgers (NL)	1969
Yogi Berra	**1946–65**	**New York Yankees (AL), New York Mets (NL)**	**1972**
Josh Gibson	1930–43	Homestead Grays Pittsburgh Crawfords, Negro Leagues	1972
Rick Ferrell	1929–47	St. Louis Browns (AL), Boston Red Sox (AL) Washington Nationals (AL)	1984
Ernie Lombardi	1931–47	Brooklyn Robins (NL), Cincinnati Reds (NL) Boston Braves (NL), New York Giants (NL)	1986
Johnny Bench	1967–83	Cincinnati Reds (NL)	1989
Carlton Fisk	1969–93	Boston Red Sox (AL), Chicago White Sox (AL)	2000

(Note: When Ozzie Smith goes into the Hall of Fame in August 2002, there will be 254 members. He is the year's only inductee.)

Shin guards were the last pieces of protective gear that catchers began to wear. They may have been borrowed from cricket batsmen and wicketkeepers.

However, in 1907, New York Giants star catcher Roger Bresnahan came out of the dugout wearing leather shin guards resembling those worn by a hockey goalie. Bresnahan's move was daring. He was the first catcher to wear this kind of protective gear out in the open. The crowd howled its disrespect, according to the *New York Times'* account of the game.

Herold "Muddy" Ruel was a lawyer who became a backstop. He caught for greats like Walter Johnson with the Washington Senators in the 1920s. Reportedly he coined the phrase "the tools of ignorance" to describe the catcher's unusual suit of armor.

Catchers' equipment continued to improve decade by decade. By the time Yogi came to the position in the mid-1930s, catching gear was fairly well-developed and standardized.

From the Hill to the Majors

Yogi Berra was born on May 12, 1925, the youngest son of Pietro and Paulina Berra. Like many others before him, Pietro left his native Italy in search of a better life in America. He settled down with other hard-working immigrants in the Little Italy section of South St. Louis, called "the Hill." He went to work in the brickyards to support his family, which had grown to four sons and a daughter.

Along with other kids in the Hill neighborhood, Yogi spent every spare moment playing ball, much to the disdain of his father, who wanted the boy to make something of himself. In fact, when Yogi got his first offer to play professional ball with the New York

This is a family portrait of the Berras taken around 1934. Yogi Berra is standing to the right of his seated father.

Yankees, Yogi's brothers John, Tony, and Mike, and his sister, Josie, had to convince Papa Berra that baseball was a worthy occupation for his son.

Lawdie (no one called him Lawrence) and neighborhood chum Joe "Joey" Garagiola played every sport imaginable—football, street hockey, basketball—but young Berra excelled at baseball. The nickname Yogi was bestowed upon him after another boy said he resembled a Hindu yogi (holy man) from a recent movie the boys had seen about India.

As a short and stocky fourteen-year-old, Yogi also tried his hand at boxing. He tested his skills in the ring at the Italian-American Club. He was pretty good, winning eight or nine bouts, most by knockout. However, when Papa Berra found out his youngest son was fighting, he made him quit. Yogi promised he would stick with baseball. Along with Joey, he alternated between pitching and catching for the Stags, the YMCA team. It was his neighborhood team, and he helped lead them to a championship.

Yogi Berra *(second row, second from right)* with neighborhood baseball friends, including Joe Garagiola *(front left)*, who would also grow up to play major league baseball.

Yogi was not a great student. He looked for every chance to play ball. He left school after eighth grade to earn money for his family, selling soft drinks, working in a shoe factory, and in the coal yards. All the while, he played American Legion ball.

Berra says in his latest book, *When You Come to a Fork in the Road, Take It!*, that leaving school was one of his first major decisions. His parents, the school principal, and the parish priest tried to talk him out of it, but he refused. "I was a lousy student and pretty stubborn and felt I was wasting my time," Yogi said. While he realizes the importance of education, Yogi never regretted the choice he made to pursue his dream of becoming a baseball player.

Yogi closely followed his hometown Cardinals and the American League cellar-dwellers, the St. Louis Browns. His favorite player was Joe Medwick of the Cards. Called "Ducky" because of the way he ran, Medwick won the National League Most Valuable Player (MVP) award and Triple Crown in 1937.

Joe Garagiola claims in his book, *It's Anybody's Ballgame*, that Yogi was, hands down, the best athlete in their neighborhood. He was also a great organizer. He was the one who got the teams together and made sure they had the proper equipment. He was the one who transformed an abandoned clay mine into a baseball field. He also painted the lines for a regulation football field, ruining Papa Berra's good paintbrush.

"He had an instinct for doing the right thing at the right time, no matter what the sport," wrote his pal Garagiola. Garagiola grew up to be a catcher, too, spending nine seasons in the majors with the Cardinals, Pirates, Cubs, and Giants before becoming a broadcaster. "He'd suggest a play—sometimes so simple we wouldn't think of it, sometimes so complicated we wouldn't understand it—and if we gave him an argument, he'd say, 'Just do it and see.' And he'd be right. Yogi wasn't loud, just sure of himself. He led by doing, and by being himself."

The best catchers during Yogi's childhood were the Yankees' Bill Dickey and the Tigers' Mickey Cochrane. Dickey later became Yogi's mentor.

Cochrane, who played from 1925 to 1937, was one of the best catchers of his era. He spent nine seasons with the Philadelphia Athletics, leading them to three straight pennants from 1929 to 1931. During those years he batted .331, .357, and .349, averaging 129 games a season. Cochrane collected 87 RBIs. He was traded in 1934 to Detroit. Cochrane was a fine defensive backstop, and one of the few catchers with a career batting average over .300. Cochrane batted over .300 nine times and finished with a career average of .320. In 1928, the American League honored him with the Most Valuable Player award after he led all catchers in putouts and hit .293 with 10 home runs and 57 RBIs. He won the MVP award again in 1934. For eleven consecutive years during the late 1920s and early 1930s, Cochrane was durable, catching over 100 games per season, which was a rarity for that position. One of Yogi's future teammates, Mickey Mantle, was actually named after Cochrane. Sadly, Cochrane's career came to an unfortunate end in 1937 after he was beaned and nearly killed by a pitch. He worked as a manager briefly, years later. But he was never the same after his son died in World War II. Cochrane was elected to the Baseball Hall of Fame in 1947.

But if anyone had any influence on Yogi Berra, it was Dickey. In 1946, Dickey played his last year with the Yankees as Berra played his first. Dickey took the rookie catcher under his wing and taught him the tricks of the trade.

William "Bill" Dickey, a catcher for the New York Yankees, during spring training in 1935.

Catching in the 1940s and 1950s was a different job from what it is today. A catcher was expected to block balls in the dirt and call a good game for the pitcher. He was required to be a talented fielder, to scoop up bunts in front of the plate, and keep base runners from stealing.

Players were not expected to be fast runners in those days. Players just didn't run as much as they do now. When Jackie Robinson came along, his speed made him notorious for stealing home. Robinson created havoc on the base paths and gave headaches to catchers like Berra.

The Road to the Majors

Yogi's journey to Cooperstown got off to a rocky start. Only a fair catcher at first, it was Yogi's batting that made the baseball scouts take notice of him.

Leo Browne, a former umpire and the manager of the Stockham American Legion Post, was one of the first people impressed by Yogi's slugging ability. Browne positioned Yogi behind the plate and in the outfield.

His batting skill hinted that the physically awkward Berra might someday be a professional ballplayer. Lacking the grace and form of a polished hitter, Berra swung at the oddest pitches. Whether they were low, high, or even outside, Berra still managed to connect with surprising power.

In 1941, when Yogi was sixteen, Browne made Yogi a full-time catcher. Browne believed that would be the best position for Yogi. He also arranged for Yogi and Joey to try out with their hometown St. Louis Cardinals.

Browne met the boys at the ballpark. He told them that Cardinals president Branch Rickey and other officials were overseeing the tryout. They would be judged on speed-of-hand, eye-hand coordination, and general skill in throwing, running, and hitting.

Yogi performed well at the plate, but several of his throws to second base were off the mark. He had a strong arm but accuracy was a problem. Garagiola easily made the cut and received a $500 signing bonus to play for the Cardinals' Springfield farm club.

When it was Yogi's turn to talk to Rickey, the Cardinals' president told Yogi that although he worked hard, he was too small and a bit wild. Yogi protested that his friend Joey had made it, and he asked Rickey if there weren't somewhere he could play. Rickey admired Yogi's courage and offered him $250 to sign. Insulted because he didn't get the same offer as Garagiola, Yogi refused. Startled, Rickey told the disconsolate Berra that he didn't think he'd ever be a major league ballplayer. Rickey said he thought Yogi would be better off getting a real job instead of wasting his time on baseball!

Undaunted, Yogi didn't quit. He continued playing for Browne's Legion team. About a year later, a scout from the New York Yankees came in search of new talent. When the scout, Johnny Schulte, a friend of Browne's, said he was looking for a hitter, Browne told him he had just the player. Yogi responded by smashing a homer, a double to right field, and a triple over the center fielder's head. Not one pitch had been in the strike zone.

Berra swings his bat during spring training in this undated photograph.

Convinced, Schulte signed the new slugger and offered Yogi the $500 bonus he had wanted. After getting the consent of his father, Yogi officially became a New York Yankee. Eighteen years old and leaving home for the first time, Berra boarded a train for Norfolk, Virginia, to play for the Yanks' Class B Piedmont League farm club. The year was 1943, and the pay was only $90 a month, but Yogi couldn't have been happier.

D–Day—A Rocket Boat in Normandy

J apan bombed Pearl Harbor in December 1941, thrusting the United States into the middle of World War II. Thousands of young men were drafted into military service, ballplayers included. There were discussions about shutting down the Major Leagues entirely. But President Franklin Delano Roosevelt strongly believed that the national pastime would help maintain the nation's morale.

The cries of "play ball" continued to echo in ballparks while about 500 major leaguers and 4,000 minor leaguers swapped their baseball flannels for the military fatigues of the U.S. Army, Navy, Coast Guard, and Marine Corps.

Pictured are three of the U.S. battleships that were bombed from the air during Japanese attacks on Pearl Harbor on December 7, 1941. Left to right: U.S.S. *West Virginia*, U.S.S. *Tennessee*, and U.S.S. *Arizona*.

As the war raged on, baseball rosters were depleted. The game's greatest stars were drafted by the Selective Service, or they enlisted. So many minor leaguers were called into service that the number of leagues in baseball's farm system dwindled from forty-four to twelve.

Many ballplayers marched off to war, including stars such as Joe DiMaggio of the Yankees, Ted Williams of the Red Sox, Stan Musial of the Cardinals, Johnny Mize of the

Giants, Mickey Cochrane and Charlie Gehringer of the Tigers, Warren Spahn of the Braves, Carl Furillo and Pee Wee Reese of the Dodgers, and Ralph Kiner of the Pirates.

When his buddy Joe Garagiola and other friends from the old neighborhood also entered the service, Yogi decided he would join the navy. After boot camp in Little Creek, Virginia, Yogi volunteered for rocket boat duty. His unit shipped out from Lido Beach, Long Island, and he found himself in the thick of the action.

Yogi was a nineteen-year-old second-class seaman when his rocket boat crew took part in the historic D-Day landing along the 50-mile stretch of fortified coastline in Normandy, France. The result of years of planning by military strategists, D-Day was the largest amphibious invasion ever attempted. On the morning of June 6, 1944, Allied forces on land, sea, and in the air attacked the German air force and the German troops who were defending the coast as part of Adolf Hitler's "Atlantic Wall," which extended from Denmark down through southern France.

Yogi Berra enlisted in the navy during World War II. He took part in the historic D-Day landings at Normandy, France.

> "Even now it brings pain to recall what happened there on June 6, 1944. I have returned many times to honor the valiant men who died on that beach. They should never be forgotten. Nor should those who lived to carry the day by the slimmest of margins. Every man who set foot on Omaha Beach that day was a hero."
>
> —**General Omar Bradley, commander of U.S. ground forces in Europe on D-Day**

By the end of the day, approximately 34,000 troops had landed at Omaha Beach. Battered but facing less resistance, British and Canadian soldiers secured the beachheads at Gold, Sword, and Juno and continued to advance inland. On Omaha Beach alone, more than 2,400 American soldiers died. Today, the American cemetery at Omaha Beach contains 9,386 gravestones.

Yogi was the only Hall of Famer who saw action at D-Day. His unit traveled from Boston to Glasgow, Scotland, on a landing ship tank (LST) to prepare for the invasion. The trip overseas was extremely rough and most of the men got sick, Yogi says in *Yogi, It Ain't Over* . . . . The crew of six men disembarked from the **U.S.S.** *Bayfield* and manned the rocket boat that was to provide cover for the Omaha Beach landing.

"Our job was to shoot at the German machine gun emplacements so our guys could have a better chance of making it to the beach," Yogi writes in his latest book, *When You Come to a Fork in the Road, Take It!* "With the bombs and the flares in the sky, it looked like fireworks on the Fourth of July. It reminded me of the holiday back home in Forest Park. I didn't know enough to be scared, so I stuck my head out, just looking up at all the colors in the sky. I was apparently watching too much for my lieutenant, who yelled at me, 'You better get your damn head down if you want to keep it!' I took his advice.

"For me, there wasn't time to be scared. I said my prayers, then we worked like the devil to load the guns, shoot them, and keep our boat moving. We must have been out there six hours until the beachhead was finally secured."

D-Day turned the tide of the war in Europe in the Allies' favor. By early September 1944, all but a fraction of France had been liberated from the Nazis. The combined forces of the American, British, and Canadian armies retook Belgium and part of the Netherlands, and reached the German frontier. The advance created by the Normandy campaign and the subsequent Battle of the Bulge in the Ardennes Forest helped the Allies gain ground in Europe and slowed the Axis powers' juggernaut.

Yogi endured another battle about a month after Normandy. This time his unit was sent to southern France.

"It wasn't really D-Day, but when they shoot at you it is D-Day, the Battle of the Bulge and Gettysburg, all rolled into one," he remembers in *Yogi, It Ain't Over* . . . . "This was on the southern coast of France and we were going to do the same thing we did at Omaha Beach. I think I was more scared this time than I was the first, but that may be because I think I should say so."

American assault troops move onto a beachhead during the D–Day invasion of German-occupied France during World War II.

Yogi's unit shelled a beach there. When the shelling ended, Yogi was struck by the reaction of the townspeople. He thought it quite amazing that after the beach was secured, hundreds of French people came out of hiding. They were so grateful to the troops who liberated their village that they presented them with flowers and bottles of wine.

Baseball stars like Ted Williams, Stan Musial, and Joe DiMaggio interrupted their careers to serve in World War II. Two major leaguers, Elmer Gedeon and Harry O'Neill, were among those ballplayers who paid the ultimate sacrifice with their lives.

Baseball accomplished its goal of keeping the country together in wartime and in peacetime. Overseas, baseball was played in every jungle or outpost where the thousands of American servicemen were stationed. Many, like DiMaggio, played on service teams that raised money for the war effort.

One interesting effect of the war-ravaged roster was that it boosted the fortunes of the St. Louis Browns. The Brownies, perennially a last-place, second-division team, captured the American League pennant in 1944. It was the only championship the franchise ever won in its short history.

As a youngster, Yogi had rooted for both the Cards and Browns, and he was in the navy when the 1944 "Streetcar Series" was played between the St. Louis Cardinals of the National League and the St. Louis Browns of the American League. "I was about as far as you can be from St. Louis that year—I was in the Navy in North Africa," Yogi recalls in his book, *When You Come to a Fork in the Road, Take It!* "But I'll always remember listening to it on armed forces radio. The war depleted both teams, but that didn't matter. To me and everyone back home, the all-St. Louis series was a big deal." Led by Stan "The Man" Musial, who had not yet entered the military, the Cards beat their cross-town rivals as the Browns batted a meager .183 during the six game series.

Three-Time MVP, Perennial All Star

Yogi hadn't played well during his first year in Norfolk. He had been behind the plate for 111 games that season, and he had batted .258. But he showed spurts of power that kept the Yankees interested, and they assigned him to their Kansas City Triple-A farm club.

After the war, Yogi reported to the New London, Connecticut, submarine base to play for the base team. He performed fairly well, so the Yankees sent him to play with the Newark Bears in the International League, where he played catcher and part-time outfielder.

Yogi's hitting impressed manager George Selkirk and the rest of the Yankee front office. In seventy-seven games against International League pitching, Berra hit .314. He connected for 15 homers and drove in 59 runs. Going into

This picture of Berra was taken when he was with the Newark Bears in 1946.
The photo is autographed, "Larry Berra."

the final week of the 1946 season, the Yankees trailed the Boston Red Sox by seventeen games. The Yankees were wallowing in third place when they brought up their new rookies.

It was September 22, 1946, when Yogi started his first Yankee game against the Philadelphia A's. He later said he was nervous. Despite Yogi's nerves, his major league debut was memorable. In addition to calling a fine game for pitcher Spud Chandler, Yogi went two for four, cracking a home run his first time at bat, driving a pitch into the right field bleachers in the fourth inning against Jessie Flores. His two-run homer won the game for the Bronx Bombers, 4–3.

Yogi stayed with the big club until season's end. He played in seven games, batted .364, and hit two home runs. He went home to St. Louis, anxious for 1947 spring training to begin.

When the new season began, Aaron Robinson and Sherman Lollar shared catching duties. Berra was assigned to the outfield, where he made errors because his throwing was erratic.

Team manager Bucky Harris knew that despite Berra's being a clumsy outfielder, he had to find Yogi a place in the batting lineup.

By the end of the 1947 season, Yogi was batting third or fourth. He had been penciled into the lineup as catcher more and more often. In 83 games, he hit .280. He had clouted 11 round-trippers, including two grand slams. He had knocked in 54 RBIs.

The Dodgers and Yanks squared off in the World Series that year. Harris surprised Berra by starting him at the plate. Weakened by an infection, Yogi was sluggish, and it showed. Responsible for several costly throwing errors, the young catcher was benched in games three and five. He was moved to the outfield for games six and seven.

At bat, Berra was a bright spot. In game three, which the Dodgers won 9–8, Yogi came up in the seventh inning and slugged a Ralph Branca pitch over the wall. He became the first player to hit a pinch-hit home run in World Series history.

Rookie Yogi Berra (number 35) slides into home plate as a ball meant for the catcher bounces off him. The Yankees beat the Washington Senators 7–0 in this 1947 match.

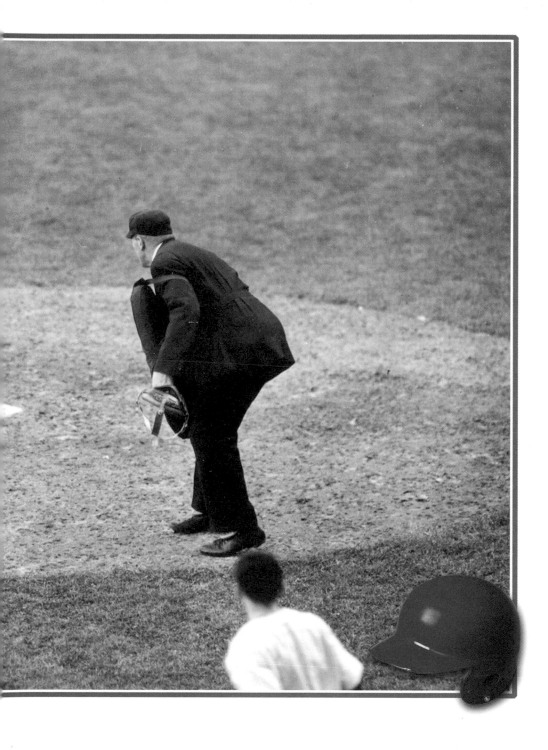

In game seven, the Yankees broke through against Brooklyn, winning 5–2. This was their eleventh World Championship. Yogi had a tough day in right field; in the second inning, he botched a line drive by Dodger Gene Hermanski and misplayed the carom into a triple.

The 1948 season went down to the wire as the Yankees, the Red Sox, and the Indians fought for the pennant. The Yankees faded down the stretch and finished third.

While his team failed to win the division, Yogi had a successful year. He played in 125 games and batted .305. He smashed 14 home runs and 98 RBIs, the third most of any Yankee. Only the great Joe DiMaggio, with 155 RBIs, and Tommy Henrich, with 100, drove in more runs than Yogi.

Yogi had played so well that year that he held out for three weeks on signing his contract at the start of the 1949 season. He wanted a raise in his $8,500 salary. Grudgingly, George Weiss, then Yankee general manager, gave in to Yogi's demands, hiking his salary to $12,500.

Right from his rookie year, Yogi knew that he was not a strong fielder. In his day, kids received no formal baseball instruction. Organized youth leagues under the direction of Little League baseball did not sprout up until the late 1940s.

"I learned baseball by instinct. Growing up, I was never really trained or coached. We never had Little League, I just did what I felt was right, even if it was swinging at a pitch at my shoetops or eyebrows," Yogi writes in *When You Come to a Fork in the Road, Take It!* "I had good natural ability as a hitter, but I never learned the fine points of catching. So when I was a young catcher in my first couple of years with the Yankees, I was clumsy and scatter-armed. My own pitchers had little confidence in me, and I couldn't blame them."

In 1949, former Boston Braves manager Casey Stengel became the Yankees manager. Stengel took an immediate liking to the sturdy backstop. Knowing Yogi needed help behind the plate, Stengel had just the answer.

Yankees manager Casey Stengel poses in this 1957 photograph. Stengel won ten pennants in twelve years with the Yankees, from 1949–1960.

"Casey was an instinctive genius—he had a great feel for things," Yogi explains in *When You Come to a Fork in the Road, Take It!* Yogi says in one of his books that Stengel was one of the first people to show that players in the bullpen and on the bench were just as important as the starting lineup. To Yogi, Stengel was a great teacher.

Yogi was grateful that Stengel had the foresight to see his future as a catcher, even though his playing was absolutely awful his first two years. At twenty-three, Berra was at a crossroads in his career. Stengel brought Bill Dickey out of retirement to help Yogi mold into a good catcher. "I had an awful lot to learn because I did everything wrong—throwing, footwork, mechanics, even my crouch was all wrong," says Yogi.

"Every day for a couple of hours, Dickey worked with me," recalls Yogi. "He worked me on all the details of catching: how to chase pop-ups, how to spot a batter's weakness, how to move my feet . . . everything. All the while, he worked on my confidence. He kept encouraging me, telling me, 'Take pride in your position. It's the best job in baseball.' He was also motivating me by reminding me there weren't many good catchers, and that once I established myself I could have a great career." Yogi knows that Dickey helped turn things around for him. Looking back, Yogi realizes that if he hadn't been tutored by Bill Dickey, he might not have lasted as long in baseball as he did.

Under Dickey's instruction, Yogi developed into a fine catcher, leading American League catchers in games-caught and chances-accepted (putouts and assists, minus errors) eight separate times. He also led the league six times in turning double plays.

Yogi became a master at handling Yankee pitchers. He was one of only four catchers to field 1.000 in an entire season, a feat he accomplished in 1958. From July 28, 1957 to May 10, 1959, he set a major league record for catching in 148 consecutive games without an error.

The injury bug bit the Yankees throughout the 1949 season, yet somehow Stengel kept the club in contention for the pennant. DiMaggio missed half the season with a heel injury. Berra was sidelined for about a month with a broken thumb on his catching hand. Yankee subs came through with flying colors.

The Boston Red Sox held a one game lead when they arrived at Yankee Stadium for the last two games of the season. The Yanks won the first game, 5–4. The next day they clinched the pennant with a 5–3 triumph.

Yogi Berra *(left)* and Joe DiMaggio were the engineers of the New York Yankees victory in the 1950 World Series and the only two sluggers to hit the ball out of the park.

In the 1949 World Series, the Yankees faced another old rival, the Brooklyn Dodgers. The results were the same as they had been in 1941 and 1947: The Yankees won. Copping their twelfth world championship by downing Brooklyn 10–6, they won in five games.

Yogi's injured thumb kept him out of Game 3, and he managed only two hits in the entire series. For the 1949 season, Yogi batted .277, stroked 20 homers, and collected 91 RBIs.

In 1950, the Yankees won ninety-eight games to nip the Tigers and Red Sox for the flag. Several players put up record numbers. Yankees shortstop Phil Rizzuto won the league's MVP, beating out Yogi, who batted .322 with 28 home runs and 124 RBIs. Incredibly, in 597 at-bats, Berra had struck out only twelve times.

That year, the Yankees had a new World Series opponent. It was the Philadelphia A's, who hadn't won a pennant since 1915. The A's, known as the Whiz Kids for their pitching and speed, were no match, however, for the Bronx Bombers. Led by the talented pitchers Allie Reynolds, Vic Raschi, Eddie Lopat, and rookie sensation Whitey Ford, the Yanks swept the A's in four straight games.

More victories came in 1951. The Yankees won the pennant, thanks to fine pitching by Reynolds and Ford, and hitting by Yogi Berra. A tight contest in the National League between the New York Giants and Brooklyn Dodgers dominated the headlines. The Giants managed to erase a 13.5 game deficit in mid-August to tie and force a three-game playoff.

The New York Giants, in what is known in baseball lore as the "Miracle of Coogan's Bluff," won the pennant. Down 4–1 to the Dodgers in the ninth, the Giants rallied. Raising the score to 4–2, they brought hard-hitting Bobby Thomson to the plate. Two runners were on base. Brooklyn's Ralph Branca came from the bullpen as a reliever. Taking strike one, Thomson clubbed the next pitch over the Polo Grounds' left field wall for the improbable playoff victory.

After Thomson's blast, the Giants ran out of miracles. They lost the World Series in six games. Yogi didn't match the statistics he had in 1950, but he played well enough to win his first MVP award.

It had been a close vote, with Yogi topping St. Louis Browns' pitcher Ned Garver and teammate Allie Reynolds to become the league's best player, according to the Baseball Writers Association of America. Berra received 184 votes. Garver received 157 votes, and Reynolds received 125. For Berra, the Most Valuable Player award was a fitting end to a great season.

Yogi, who finished the season batting .294, led the Yanks in slugging with 88 RBIs and 27 homers. He was becoming a true Bronx Bomber. Between 1949 and 1955, he was the heart of the Yankee batting order, leading his team in RBIs each year.

The 1951 season was special for another reason. Yogi had been behind the plate for two of Reynolds's no-hitters. On July 12, 1951, Reynolds bested Cleveland's Bob Feller with a 1–0 no-hitter. Later that year, on September 28, Reynolds blanked the Red Sox 8–0 in the first game of a double bill. Berra almost cost Reynolds the shutout when he dropped a foul pop hit in the ninth. But he redeemed himself and preserved Reynolds's historic game by catching the next pitch, which popped up near the dugout.

Fresh off his MVP year, Yogi started the 1952 season $7,000 richer when general manager George Weiss raised his salary to $35,000. Yogi, who loved to hold out during spring training as a negotiating tactic, reported to training camp on time.

A catcher, says Yogi, in *When You Come to a Fork in the Road, Take It!*, has to be smart and physically skilled. "I developed a good throwing arm and had a blocky body, which is good for a catcher. But I really used my brain more than anything. As a catcher, you scrounge for every edge. A thousand things happen in a game, little things, and you have to keep those things in your head. In the 1953 World Series, I threw two runners out at third base on back-to-back bunts. People thought I stole the Dodgers' signs. Truth is, I was watching how the batters' feet were pointed, and how our pitcher was keeping the ball where I wanted it. I could just tell the bunts were going to the left of the plate—and that's where they went."

For the first time in his career, Yogi occupied the cleanup spot, and he didn't disappoint. He hit .273, and blasted 30 homers. He knocked in 98 runs.

Despite a slow start, the Yankees rallied in the second half of the season to capture their fourth straight pennant. They were led by Berra and a shy Oklahoma farm boy—a power hitter named Mickey Charles Mantle who had

Billy Martin *(second from left)* gets a hug from Coach Frank Crosetti (number 2) after Martin drove in the winning run, clinching the 1953 World Series for the Yankees, their fifth consecutive Series' win.

replaced DiMaggio in center field. Mantle went on to hit 536 career home runs.

The Yankees' domination of the Dodgers continued in the World Series as they defeated them in seven games. Yogi contributed two homers and three RBIs, but he batted only .214.

The Yankees soared to a fifth straight championship in 1953. Who would they face in the World Series? It was Brooklyn once more.

Yogi was again the cornerstone of the Yankee offense. He batted .296, smashed 27 home runs, and pounded in 108 runs. Yogi literally drove the Dodgers batty during the World Series. In six games, he hit a sizzling .429 with one home run and four RBIs.

In 1954, the Yankee's string of World Series appearances was halted when the Indians reached a record-setting 111 wins. The Bronx Bombers won 103 games, finishing eight games behind Cleveland.

While denied another championship ring, Yogi won his second American League MVP award. He beat out the Indians' Larry Doby and Bobby Avila, who finished second and third in the voting, respectively. Yogi caught for all but five games. His batting average was .307, with 22 home runs and 125 RBIs.

In 1955, Yogi repeated as league MVP, narrowly edging out Detroit's Al Kaline. While his batting average had dropped to .272, he had smashed 27 homers and 108 RBIs. Yogi had delivered key hits to help the Yankees reach the World Series again.

With the revival of the Subway Series, the Yankees received a thrashing from their old nemesis, the Brooklyn Dodgers. It was revenge for all the Yankees' victories of past years.

Two plays had set the tone for the Series. Dodger Jackie Robinson stole home on Berra in the first game although Yogi still insists that Robinson was out at the plate. Outfielder Sandy Amoros robbed Yogi with a spectacular one-handed running catch in the sixth inning of Game 7, saving the game and the championship for Brooklyn.

Catching Perfection

During the 1956 season, Yogi enjoyed one of his greatest thrills in baseball. Relying on the potent batting of Hank Bauer, Gil McDougald, Mantle, and Berra, the Yankees breezed to their twenty-second pennant. Yogi batted .298, with 30 home runs and 105 RBIs. He was second to Mantle, who had a career MVP year.

The Dodgers looked forward to their rematch with the Yankees in the World Series. They were hoping to win their second consecutive title.

Brooklyn jumped out to a two-game lead. But Yankee ace Whitey Ford took one back with a 5–3 victory in Game 3. The Yankees rolled to a 6–2 win in Game 4.

The pivotal fifth game loomed large. Journeyman pitcher Don Larsen was on the mound for the Yankees. Larsen had an 11–5 record

Yogi Berra (number 8) jumps into the arms of pitcher Don Larsen after Larsen pitched the first, and only, perfect game in World Series history to date, shutting out the Brooklyn Dodgers 2–0 in 1956.

that year, but he had gotten shelled in the second game with a 13–8 loss.

Larsen threw 97 pitches. He ran the count to three balls on only one of the 27 batters. Striking out seven, he was helped out by Mantle's fourth-inning homer which had given him the lead. Mantle's running backhanded catch of a Gil Hodges's line drive preserved the no-hitter.

Third baseman Andy Carey also came through with two fine fielding plays. The Dodgers sent up pinch hitter Dale Mitchell as the last batter. Mitchell took one ball and one strike. He struck at a low curve to bring the count to 1–2.

Larsen was one pitch away from a no-hitter. Nerves set in. He stepped off the mound to compose himself.

Mitchell fouled off the next pitch. Then Larsen deposited a letter-high fastball into Berra's glove. Strike three! Berra jumped into Larsen's waiting arms. Together they jumped into the record books.

Berra had an impressive series at bat, too. He compiled a .360 average with 10 RBIs.

"When people ask me what my biggest thrill was, I always say catching Don Larsen's perfect game in the 1956 World Series was right up there," Yogi explains in his book. "That's because it happened in the high drama of a World Series. And against such a powerful team, the Brooklyn Dodgers. As the catcher, I was pretty calm—I was so concentrated on calling a good game—but I was pretty nervous going into that last inning.

"And Don's palms were sweaty, too. The game was still close, we were only winning 2–0, and I didn't want to worry him about the perfect game. Nobody said anything to Larsen all game for fear of jinxing him. But before the ninth inning, I told him, 'Let's get the first guy. That's the main thing.' And Gooney Bird—that's what we called him—did just that and even better. He made history and all hell broke loose."

—Yogi Berra
When You Come to a Fork in the Road, Take It!

Berra hit a grand slam in Game 2. Crushing two more homers in the deciding seventh game, he helped the Yanks clinch their seventeenth World Series title.

The 1957 season began quietly. But baseball purists were shocked and saddened when news came during the season that both the beloved Brooklyn Dodgers and the New York Giants were moving west to California after the season.

Berra didn't have a particularly good year, either. He struggled, hitting only .251 for the season, with 24 homers and 82 RBIs. It was a big drop from the 105 runs he drove in the year before. However, he was steady behind the plate. For the fourth straight year, he had led American League catchers in putouts, with 704. Mantle won his second consecutive MVP award as the Yankees won 98 games, and beat the White Sox for their eighth pennant in nine years.

The Bronx Bombers faced the Milwaukee Braves in the 1957 World Series. The Hank Aaron–led squad upset the champs in seven games. Yogi batted .320 in the Series, with one homer. He was outdone by Hammerin' Hank. Aaron is baseball's all-time home run leader. Aaron, who went on to amass 755 homers, hit a blistering .393 with three homers in the

Series. Lew Burdette pitched three complete game victories for the Braves.

Teammates Mantle, Ford, and Billy Martin were notorious for enjoying New York's nightlife. The trio partied regularly after games. Sometimes they went overboard. Many times Mantle or Ford played while sick or drunk if they had stayed out all night before a game.

Off the field, Yogi was a family man. Occasionally, though, he celebrated the success of his team. One of the most publicized incidents surrounding Yogi and his teammates took place in May 1957. A group of Yankees and some of their wives had gone to the Copacabana nightclub in New York to celebrate Martin's twenty-ninth birthday.

A delicatessen owner, claiming that Yankee Hank Bauer slugged him, filed a $250,000 lawsuit. The six players who had been involved were each fined $1,000. Berra and Ford were benched for the next game. Although the case was eventually thrown out of court, Billy Martin, who was accused of being a trouble-maker, was traded to Kansas City.

Mickey Mantle, Billy Martin and Hank Bauer and his wife stand outside the New York City Criminal Courts building after Bauer was cleared in the Copacabana case.

While the Copacabana incident created an uproar, Yogi believed the players were brought closer together as a result. The Yankees were stuck in third place and six games out when the fight occurred. After seven straight wins, the Bombers recaptured first place and eventually won the pennant.

Berra's worst year in the majors resulted in his first-ever pay cut. He signed for $58,000 to start the 1958 season. It was $2,500 less than he had made the year before. His batting average had dropped. He had tried wearing glasses during the year to correct his poor eyesight. Eventually he discarded the glasses on the advice of his wife.

The Yankees easily won the 1958 pennant by ten games, but runs were down significantly. No Yankee had over 100 runs batted in. Yogi, who hit a meager .266, slipped to 90 RBIs.

In the 1958 World Series, the Yankees found themselves in a rematch with the Braves. Behind the pitching of Warren Spahn and Lew Burdette, Milwaukee streaked out to a 3–1 Series lead. Things looked grim for the Bronx Bombers. Strong Yankee pitching kept the series alive and brought them to a decisive seventh game. The score was tied 2–2 in the eighth when Yogi ignited the critical game-winning rally. He had doubled into the right corner. Four runs later, the Yankees were once again the champs!

One of Yogi's charms as a player was that he loved to talk and annoy opposing hitters. He chatted incessantly about the game, his family, the weather—anything, in an attempt to distract the batter.

Hall of Famer Hank Aaron remembers this exchange with Yogi during the 1958 World Series. Yogi kept telling Aaron to "hit with the label up on the bat." Finally, Aaron turned around and said, "Yogi, I came up here to hit, not to read."

During the 1959 season, Yogi and his teammates found themselves in unfamiliar territory. Having trailed the Chicago White Sox most of the season, for part of the year, they even languished in the basement! Despite a late season surge, the Yankees uncharacteristically finished third. They were fifteen games behind the Go-Go Sox, as they were called that year. Yogi had batted .284 and had driven in 69 runs that season. While his 19 home runs were a career low, he reached a milestone by hitting his 300th homer on August 9 in a game against Kansas City.

On September 19, 1959, the Yankees celebrated their future Hall of Famer on Yogi Berra Day. Among the gifts the lovable catcher received were golf and fishing equipment, trips to Italy and Bermuda, a new station wagon, redwood furniture, a color TV, a swimming pool, a pool table, and dance lessons.

Yogi Berra Career Statistics

AVG =.285	HR = 358
G = 2120	RBI = 1430
AB = 7555	BB = 704
R = 1175	K = 414
H = 2150	OBP = .348
2B = 321	SLG = .482
3B = 49	

- Played from 1946–1965,
- New York Yankees (AL), Catcher/OF
- Manager, New York Yankees (AL) 1964, 1984–85
- Manager, New York Mets (NL), 1972–75.
- Three-time MVP in 1951, 1954, and 1955
- Probably the only manager to have led AL and NL teams to the pennant, the 1964 Yankees and the 1973 Mets.
- Held the career home-run record for AL catchers until topped by Carlton Fisk, who popped 351 homers as catcher in 24 major league seasons.
- Topped 100 RBI mark four years in a row.
- His 14 pennants and 10 world championships top all other players.
- Played in 75 World Series games, compiling .274 average, 12 HRs, and 39 RBIs.
- Compiled 484-444 record as a manager, a .522 winning percentage.

Meanwhile, the Dodgers had moved to Los Angeles. They overpowered the Sox in six games to win their first West Coast title.

The Berra Family

The one constant in Yogi's life has always been family. He was devoted to his parents, and he has been married to Carmen, the love of his life, for more than fifty years. They met when Yogi was a rookie catcher with the Yankees. Carmen was a waitress at Biggie's Restaurant in St. Louis. Yogi was awkward and shy around women. He was afraid she wouldn't go out with him. Once Yogi finally got the nerve to ask her out, they began dating. Joe Garagiola served as the best man at Yogi's wedding. Yogi returned the favor when Garagiola married his wife, Audrie.

Carmen and Yogi were married on January 26, 1949, in St. Louis. Making $12,000 a year, Yogi supplemented their income in the off-season by working as a headwaiter at Ruggiero's Restaurant in his hometown.

Carmen and Yogi were married in St. Louis on January 26, 1949.

Carmen was eager to start a family. Yogi knew there would be more opportunities for work if they moved to the New York area. They left St. Louis in 1951. Eventually they settled in Montclair, New Jersey, where the family still lives.

Larry Jr. was the first-born of their children. He was followed by Tim and Dale. The three boys idolized their father. They spent a lot of time around the Yankee clubhouse. Yogi was on the road so much that Carmen often had to be both a mother and a father to the boys.

Larry loved baseball and wanted to go professional right out of high school. He was talked into going to college first. Unfortunately, Larry was injured while playing at Montclair State. He signed with the Mets, but didn't make it very far in the minor leagues.

Tim says that he was probably the best ballplayer in the family, but he didn't want the pressure of following after his famous father. He turned to football. After starring at the University of Massachusetts, he signed with the Baltimore Colts as a wide receiver, playing for them during the 1974 season.

Yogi shares a smile with his son Dale, who played for the New York Yankees thirty years after his father.

Despite comparisons to his Hall of Fame father, Dale Berra made it to the majors on his own. An above-average infielder, he was drafted by the Pittsburgh Pirates in 1975. A utility player at third base and shortstop, Dale stayed with the Pirates from 1977 to 1984. He was traded to the Yankees to start the 1985 season. He finished his career with the Houston Astros in 1987.

Dale Berra Career Statistics

Played from 1977–1987

Pittsburgh Pirates (NL),

1977–1984

New York Yankees (AL),

1985–1986

Houston Astros (NL), 1987, SS/Third Baseman

AVG= .236	HR = 49
G = 853	RBI = 278
AB = 2553	BB = 210
R = 236	K = 422
H = 603	OBP = .297
2B = 109	SLG = .344
3B = 9	

"I knew I could never be as good as my dad," Dale said about his eleven years in the majors. "I had some huge shoes to fill. If I hadn't been Yogi Berra's son, I would have been a better than average big league infielder. Would I have it that way? The answer of course is no."

Dale and Yogi held the father-son record for home runs at 407 before Bobby and Barry Bonds broke the mark in 1989.

In 1985, Yogi was a manager for the New York Yankees. It was a proud moment for Yogi when he was able to coach his son. This family affair only lasted sixteen games. Yogi was fired and replaced by Billy Martin.

Yogi and Carmen pose with their children and grandchildren in 1998.

Family life has always been important to Yogi. He loves being at home, doting on his nine grandchildren. The courtship that began in 1947 with Carmen developed into a lifelong friendship. Yogi speaks affectionately about their marriage in *When You Come to a Fork in the Road, Take It!* "What can I say about Carmen, except that she's still beautiful and intelligent and has put up with a lot being married to me for over fifty years. It isn't easy being a ballplayer's wife, especially when you're in charge of three young boys at home. But Carm's been my partner the whole time, and believe me, her sacrifices and support were truly vital to my baseball career."

Life Off
the Field

In 1960, Mickey Mantle and Roger Maris powered the Yankees to 97 victories as they outpaced the Baltimore Orioles to win their twenty-fifth pennant. Yogi was switched to the outfield for most of the year to give his thirty-five-year-old body a rest. While he batted .276, hit 15 homers, and drove in 62 runs, he was still a tough out.

In the World Series that year, the National League champion Pittsburgh Pirates proved their mettle. After six games, the Bucs and Yanks were tied. This forced a final game at Forbes Field in Pittsburgh. The game turned into a slugfest. The Pirates held a slim 9–7 lead before the Yankees came through to tie in the top of the ninth inning. Pirate Bill Mazeroski stepped in against pitcher Ralph Terry. The game was on the line.

In a dramatic confrontation that only the World Series could bring, Mazeroski crushed Terry's third pitch over the left field wall for the game-winning home run. Yogi felt helpless as he watched the ball go over his head.

The team's failure to win in 1960 was blamed on the players who spent too much time celebrating after games. It cost manager Casey Stengel his job. That same situation would later play into Yogi's career as a manager.

In 1961, Yogi moved to the outfield permanently. Expansion had changed baseball's alignment. Two new teams, the Los Angeles Angels and the Washington Senators, joined the American League. The '61 season featured a memorable home-run race. Maris and Mantle became embroiled in a bitter battle to beat Babe Ruth's sixty home-run record. Maris finally broke the barrier. His record of 61 homers stood for thirty-seven years. It was eclipsed in 1998. Mark McGwire of the Cardinals hit 70 out of the park, but his record didn't last. Giants slugger Barry Bonds erased McGwire's mark in 2001 by hitting 73 homers.

Yankees teammates and home-run rivals Roger Maris *(left)* and Mickey Mantle look at a seemingly endless telegram from enthusiastic fans.

The Yankees won 109 games that season. They won the pennant by eight games. Yogi batted .271 on the year, hitting 22 homers, and driving in 61 runs. The Yanks nabbed the World Series against Cincinnati in five games. Berra missed one game with a shoulder injury, but he managed to hit .273 with one home run and three RBIs.

The next season, 1962, Berra continued in a part-time role by playing 59 games in the field. He was thirty-seven-years old. The Yankees no longer relied on his bat to win. Yogi's production had dropped significantly. He knocked in 35 runs and hit .224, with ten homers.

In the 1962 World Series the Yanks met an old foe, the Giants, who now called the city of San Francisco home. The Giants streaked to a two-game lead. The Yankees rallied behind clutch pitching and timely hitting by Clete Boyer to win their twentieth world championship.

Yankee pitching dominated the 1963 season, and they got the flag by 10.5 games over Chicago. Yogi was in his last full season, playing 64 games. His average was a respectable .293. But he drove in a mere 28 runs, with eight homers.

The Yankees faced the Los Angeles Dodgers in the 1963 World Series. Pitchers Sandy Koufax and Don Drysdale silenced Yankee bats as the Dodgers won in four straight games.

After the stinging defeat, the Yankees' front office decided that a new manager might help. To start the 1964 season, Yogi replaced manager Ralph Houk. His first chance behind the bench, he accepted a pay cut to get the job. He wanted to make the most of it.

Yogi Berra poses at the 1964 spring training camp in Florida after joining the Yankees as manager.

Yogi expected his players to play as hard as he had. He didn't tolerate lack of effort. The players seemed to like him. But deep down, they didn't respect his ability as a manager.

The Yankees struggled for the first four months of the season. In August, they found themselves mired in third place. A confrontation on the team bus between Yogi and infielder Phil Linz strangely reversed the team's sagging fortunes. Upset because Linz was playing a harmonica in the midst of a four-game losing streak, Yogi scolded him for his revelry. He batted the musical instrument away. Linz was fined $200. The "harmonica incident" had long-lasting effects on team harmony.

The Yankees rallied down the stretch to win the pennant by one game. Yogi was happy to face his hometown Cardinals in the 1964 World Series. The series went to the seventh game. Four Yankee errors led to a 7–5 defeat and heartbreak. But Yogi was pleased with his performance.

It was reported in the press that players took advantage of Yogi's good nature and that he couldn't control the swimming pool parties and other forms of late-night carousing. Management blamed Yogi for failing to discipline players. They wanted him to stop their off-the-field antics.

Three days after the season, Yogi was fired. He was replaced by former Cardinals skipper Johnny Keane.

In 1965, the expansion New York Mets gave Yogi a second chance. He was hired as a player-coach at an annual salary of $40,000. In the early 1960s the lovable Mets were baseball's

Yogi *(right)* poses with New York Mets president George Weiss at the Mets' offices at Shea Stadium after being named the team's coach.

worst team. The National League franchise only won 40 games in 1962, setting a new record for futility. The Mets won 50 games and lost 112 in Yogi's first year in the coaching box. By 1968, the Mets managed to get 73 wins against 89 losses.

In 1969, Yogi Berra proved that anything can and does happen in baseball. The "Amazing Mets" overcame a 9.5 game deficit in early August to beat out Chicago for the pennant.

In the World Series, the Mets faced the American League's Baltimore Orioles. The powerful Orioles had won 109 games. The Amazing Mets surprised the baseball world by beating the favored Orioles in five games. It was the Mets' first world title!

Days before the start of the 1972 season, Mets manager Gil Hodges suffered a fatal heart attack. A grieving Yogi agreed to take over the team. Backed by the nucleus of that pennant-winning team three years earlier, he led the Mets to their second flag in 1973. He became the first manager to lead teams in both leagues to championships.

Yogi rejoined the Yankees as a coach in 1976, just as the Bronx Bombers were rounding into championship form. And he could have said "it's déjà vu all over again" when the Yankees brought him back as their manager in 1984.

They finished the season in a disappointing third place. Yogi didn't escape the wrath of controversial Yankee owner George Steinbrenner, who seems to have a revolving door when it comes to hiring and firing managers.

Steinbrenner canned Yogi just sixteen games into the 1985 season. So began a fourteen-year feud between the two men. Yogi refused invitations to Old Timers events. He would not appear at any games at Yankee Stadium with Steinbrenner in charge. In 1999, the two men finally patched up their differences. Yogi was welcomed back as a member of the Yankee family.

The Yankees commemorated his return by holding a second Yogi Berra Day on July 18, 1999. Yankee David Cone celebrated the occasion by pitching a perfect game, the third in team history.

After Baseball

Yogi retired at age sixty-four following the 1989 season as a coach with the Houston Astros. He wanted to spend more time with his family and grandchildren. After twenty-four years of baseball, he took off his cap and turned his attention to golf.

Yogi, a shrewd businessman, was the spokesman and part owner of Yoo-Hoo, a popular chocolate soft drink. In 1958, he joined

Yogi and Yankees owner George Steinbrenner parted on a good note after ending their fourteen-year feud. Yogi quipped: "Fourteen years, I'd say, is long enough. He apologized again."

with teammate Phil Rizzuto to open a forty-lane bowling center in Clifton, New Jersey, which he later sold.

Late in his career, he partnered with son Tim in managing a health and racquetball club in Fairfield, New Jersey. The club still exists under different ownership.

Yogi had many endorsement contracts, appearing in a number of commercials. He even played a brain surgeon on a television soap opera.

Today, he remains a marketing icon. Coors Brewing Company uses Yogi and his famous slogans to market its beer.

Perhaps one of his greatest achievements came in 1972, when he was inducted into the National Baseball Hall of Fame. Yogi missed induction in 1971, falling twenty-eight votes short of the required 75 percent he needed to be elected. In 1972, he received enough ballots to join the Dodgers' Sandy Koufax and Early Wynn, a pitcher with Washington, Cleveland, and Chicago, in the Hall of Fame. Koufax garnered 344 votes. Berra received 339 and Wynn collected 301.

Yogi's career is full of milestones and honors. He played in fifteen All Star games. He holds the major league record for winning 10 world championships. He appeared in a record 75 World Series games, accumulating 71 hits, 12 homers, 39 RBIs, and a .274 batting average.

Other honors followed. In May 1996, he became Dr. Lawrence Peter Berra when nearby Montclair State University bestowed

Yogi receives an honorary doctorate from Montclair State University in New Jersey in 1996

an honorary doctoral degree upon him. The university also named its new $10 million stadium complex after him. The Yogi Berra Stadium on the Montclair State campus is the home of the minor league New Jersey Jackals baseball team. In 1999, Yogi was named to Major League Baseball's All Century team, composed of the game's greatest players.

How many Hall of Famers have their own museums? Well, Yogi does. In October

Yogi admires the glove with which he caught the perfect World Series game. The glove is now housed in the Yogi Berra Museum at Montclair State University.

1998, he opened the Yogi Berra Museum and Learning Center at Montclair State. The museum displays permanent and rotating exhibits about baseball. It details Yogi's long career as a player, manager, entrepreneur, and best-selling author. Throughout the year, there are photographic and audiovisual exhibits as well as educational seminars at the museum. Berra has raised over $1 million for charity. He sponsors an annual celebrity golf tournament to benefit scouting and children with special needs.

Yogi's unique philosophy still serves him. "I learned a lot about handling pressure by playing in all those World Series. Basically, I learned to relax," Yogi has said. He admits that in a World Series game, emotions are intense and people are intense. But Yogi wouldn't let himself think about the pressure. Instead, he concentrated on his job and had fun doing it.

Yogi says he was able to block out all the hysteria about a Subway Series, which he played so many times against Brooklyn. Even though New York City went crazy when the Yankees played the Dodgers, to Yogi, it was fun. "The biggest lesson I learned about World Series pressure was simple," says Yogi in *When You Come to a Fork in the Road, Take It!* "You can't be afraid of making a mistake. There's always the next inning, or the next day. Life goes on."

As Yogi himself might say, those are good words to live by.

I Really Didn't Say Everything I Said

Yogi readily admits that he doesn't know why he says the unusual things he says, but in some strange way his homespun sayings actually make sense. A popular speaker on the banquet circuit, he is the author of four books—*Yogi, It Ain't Over . . .*; *Yogi Berra's Baseball Book: The Game and How to Play It*; *The Yogi Book: I Really Didn't Say Everything I Said*; and *When You Come to a Fork in the Road, Take It!* The last two titles chronicle his favorite Yogi-isms.

Longtime friend Joe Garagiola wrote about Yogi in *It's Anybody's Ballgame*. "His funny way of talking is actually full of common sense, just succinct, plain-people talk. It's his way of looking at things. He may take a different road to get where he's going, but you'll see that his route is usually the fastest and the most honest."

Some people think the Yogi phenomenon was started in 1946. A reporter who had covered the colorful catcher since Berra was a rookie began printing some of the things he heard him

Wisdom from Yogi

It ain't over 'til it's over.

It's déjà vu all over again.

You can observe a lot by watching.

A nickel ain't worth a dime anymore.

Nobody goes there anymore. It's too crowded.

Always go to other people's funerals,
    or they won't go to yours.

The other team could make trouble
    for us if they win.

We were overwhelming underdogs.

We're lost but we're making good time!

I usually take a two-hour nap from 1 to 4.

Never answer an anonymous letter.

say. He may or may not have tweaked some of Yogi's words. While over the years, many reporters may have embellished Yogi's statements, people have enjoyed using Yogi-isms.

Mickey Mantle recalls in *My Favorite Summer 1956* how Billy Martin locked his keys in a car. Yogi, as straight-faced as ever, offered this advice. "That's easy," said Yogi to Martin. "You gotta get a blacksmith."

This plaque commemorates Yogi Berra's induction into the Baseball Hall of Fame in 1972.

Teammate Phil Rizzuto, who roomed with Yogi, has this to say in *Yogi, It Ain't Over . . .* about Yogispeak. "I don't need to tell you that Yogi was a natural hitter and a quick learner . . . a lot of people made a bundle of money telling Yogi Berra stories at banquets during the off-season. Most of what they said was made up."

Teammates and opponents alike always had something to say about Yogi. Mantle swore that Yogi was the best clutch hitter he ever saw because "he'd swing at everything."

Ted Williams, perhaps the game's greatest hitter, acknowledged that Yogi didn't look like a hitter, but he certainly could hit.

In *Yogi, It Ain't Over . . .* Williams says, "Bill Dickey was an impressive looking guy, and here was Yogi. Well, he just didn't look like he should be a New York Yankee. I will tell you this, I never saw anyone like him. He looked like hell, but what happened when he attacked the ball was right out of a computer. He could move the runner, and move him late in the game like no one else I ever saw play the game."

YOGI BERRA *TIMELINE*

	1925	Yogi is born in St. Louis, MO.
	1941	Attack on Pearl Harbor, United States enters World War II.
	1944	Yogi sees action at D-Day.
	1946	Yogi's Rookie Year with the Yankees.
	1949	Yogi and Carmen get married.
	1951	Yogi wins his first AL MVP award.
	1954	Yogi wins his second MVP award.
	1955	Yogi wins his third MVP award.
	1956	Catches Don Larsen's Perfect World Series game.
	1961	Baseball expansion changes the game.
	1963	Yogi plays his last full season.

⚾	**1964**	Yogi manages the Yankees for the first time; he wins the pennant but is fired.
⚾	**1965**	Becomes coach for NY Mets.
⚾	**1972**	Yogi is inducted into the Baseball Hall of Fame.
⚾	**1973**	Manages the Mets to the NL flag.
⚾	**1984**	Joins Yankee staff as manager.
⚾	**1985**	Fired as Yankee manager.
⚾	**1986**	Hired as coach for Houston Astros.
⚾	**1989**	Yogi officially retires from baseball.
⚾	**1996**	Call him Dr. Yogi Berra now.
⚾	**1998**	Yogi Berra Museum opens at Montclair State University in New Jersey.

Glossary

ace Equivalent to a run under the Knickerbocker rules in the early days of baseball.
Today, ace also refers to the best pitcher on
a pitching staff.

Allied powers Great Britain, the United
States, Canada, Belgium, France, the
Netherlands, Poland, Yugoslavia, and
later the Soviet Union, as joined together
to defeat the Axis powers during World
War II.

American League The junior circuit of
professional baseball that began in 1901.
Today, the American League is divided into
three divisions: East, Central, and West. All
together, there are fourteen teams.

Axis powers During World War II, Germany,
Italy, and Japan. Bulgaria, Romania,
Finland, and Hungary also fought to aid the
German government.

backstop A common term used for catcher.

batting average The number of a player's hits divided by his or her times at bat. A good batter hits near .300 or higher. The last player to hit over .400 during an entire season was Ted Williams of the Red Sox. He batted .406 in 1941.

beaned When a player is struck in the head by a beanball, an illegal pitch. The pitcher is ejected if a player is beaned.

bon mots A French term meaning "good words." A clever remark or witticism.

cricket A British game from which baseball is thought to have originated. Cricket is played with a ball and flat-faced bat. Two teams of eleven players each meet on a large field that centers on two wickets, each defended by a batsman who hits the ball and crosses to the other wicket to score a run.

D-Day Military jargon for the day on which a military attack is scheduled to take place. D-Day, in popular usage, is associated with the June 6, 1944, invasion of Normandy by the Allies during World II.

disconsolate The feeling of being dejected, downcast, or unhappy.

icon An object of devotion or a person who is admired in society.

juggernaut A massive force, movement, or object that crushes whatever is in its path.

Knickerbocker rules The rules developed by Alexander Joy Cartwright and adopted by the New York Knickerbocker Base Ball Club on September 23, 1845, that established the layout of a diamond-shaped field with bases an equal distance apart. The rules designated nine players, set guidelines for strikes and balls, and gave power to the umpire to resolve disputes. They became the standard by which baseball's modern rules were established.

National League The first group of baseball teams to be paid. The National League is divided into three separate divisions. Sixteen teams compete for the pennant and the right to play against the American League winner in the World Series.

passed ball A pitch that is dropped by the catcher, allowing a runner to advance to the next base.

perfect game A game during which no batter has safely reached base and there are no walks. Berra caught the only World Series perfect game on October 8, 1956, when the Yankees played against the Brooklyn Dodgers.

putout A play in which a fielder catches the ball to make an out.

rounders An English game that is played with a ball and a bat. It resembles baseball.

tools of ignorance A term used to describe protective equipment worn by catchers, first coined by Herold "Muddy" Ruel, Washington Senators catcher in the 1920s. It implied that a catcher was dumb to play the most dangerous position in baseball.

town ball A variation of rounders played primarily in the New England area.

World Series The championship of modern professional baseball, first played in 1903.

Each fall, the best National League team faces off against the best American League team for the world title. The New York Yankees are often thought of as the team in all sports with the most victories. The Yanks have won thirty-eight pennants and twenty-six World Series championships in their ninety-nine year history.

yogi A mystic who is revered in the Hindu religion. Also refers to a person who practices yoga.

For More Information

The Babe Ruth Birthplace and Baseball
Center
216 Emory Street
Baltimore, MD 21230
(410) 727-1539
e-mail: lauriew@baberuthmuseum.com

The Bob Feller Hometown Museum
P.O. Box 95
310 Mill Street
Van Meter, IA 50261
(515) 996-2806
e-mail: info@bobfellermuseum.org

Major League Baseball Players Association
12 East 49th Street
New York, NY 10017
(212) 826-0808
Web site: http://bigleaguers.yahoo.com/

The National Baseball Hall of Fame
   and Museum
P.O. Box 590
25 Main St.
Cooperstown, NY 13326
(607) 547-7200
Web site: http://www.baseballhalloffame.org

The Office of the Commissioner
Major League Baseball
245 Park Avenue
New York, NY 10167
(212) 931-7800
Web site: http://www.mlb.com

Society for American Baseball Research (SABR)
812 Huron Road, Suite 719
Cleveland, OH 44115

(216) 575-0500

e-mail: info@sabr.org

The Yogi Berra Museum and Learning Center
Montclair State University
8 Quarry Road
Little Falls, NJ 07424
(973) 655-2377
e-mail: yogi.museum@montclair.edu

Videos

Burns, Ken, director. *Baseball: The National Pastime*, PBS Home Video, 1994.

Web Sites

Due to the changing nature of Internet links, the Rosen Publishing Group, Inc., has developed an online list of Web sites related to the subject of this book. This site is updated regularly. Please use this link to access the list:

http://www.rosenlinks.com/bbhf/yobe/

For Further Reading

Astor, Gerald. *The Baseball Hall of Fame, 50th Anniversary Book*. New York: Simon & Schuster, 1992.

Bedingfield, Gary. *Baseball in World War II Europe*. Charleston, SC: Arcadia Publishing, 2000.

Berra, Yogi. *The Yogi Book: I Really Didn't Say Everything I Said*. New York: Workman Publishing Company 1998.

Berra, Yogi, with Dave Kaplan. *When You Come to a Fork in the Road, Take It!* New York: Hyperion Publishing, 2001.

Berra, Yogi, with Tom Horton. *Yogi, It Ain't Over . . .* New York: McGraw-Hill Publishing Company, 1989.

Bliven, Bruce Jr. *The Story of D-Day: June 6, 1944.* New York: Random House, 1956.

Moffi, Larry. *This Side of Cooperstown: An Oral History of Major League Baseball in the 1950s.* Iowa City, IA: University of Iowa Press, 1996.

Neft, David S., and Richard M. Cohen. *The Sports Encyclopedia: Baseball.* New York: St. Martin's Press, 1995.

Okrent, Daniel, and Steve Wulf. *Baseball Anecdotes.* New York: Oxford University Press, 1989.

Yogi Berra: An American Original. Champaign, IL: Sports Publishing Inc., 2001.

Bibliography

Anderson, Dave, Murray Chass, Robert Creamer, and Harold Rosenthal. *The Yankees: The Four Fabulous Eras of Baseball's Most Famous Team.* New York: Random House, 1979.

Garagiola, Joe. *It's Anybody's Ballgame.* New York: Contemporary Books, 1988.

Mantle, Mickey, and Phil Pepe. *Mickey Mantle, My Favorite Summer 1956.* New York: Doubleday, 1991.

Roswell, Gene. *The Yogi Berra Story.* New York: Julian Messner Inc., 1958.

Turner, Frederick. *When the Boys Came Back: Baseball and 1946.* New York: Henry Holt and Company Inc., 1996.

Ward, Geoffrey C., and Kenneth Burns. *Baseball, an Illustrated History.* New York: Alfred A. Knopf, 1994.

Index

About the Author

Debra A. Estock is a writer and editor at a New York City-based trade newspaper and magazine. She remembers the first time her dad took her out in the yard and tried to get her to hit a wiffle ball over the garage. She lives with her family in New Jersey.

Photo Credits

Cover © Bettmann/Corbis; p. 4 © Hulton Archive/Getty; p. 6 © Topps Company; pp. 8, 26, 33, 39, 46–47, 50, 58, 62, 67, 80, 82, 84, 87 © AP/Wide World Photos; pp. 14, 53 © Bettmann/Corbis; pp. 20, 22, 30, 35, 43, 72, 74, 76 © Yogi Berra Museum and Learning Center; pp. 89, 90 © Mike Derer/AP/Wide World Photos; p. 94 © National Baseball Hall of Fame Library, Cooperstown, New York.

Editor

Jill Jarnow

Series Design and Layout

Geri Giordano